D0713168

PRIMARY SOURCES OF
FAMOUS PEOPLE IN AMERICAN HISTORY™

FRANCISCA ALVAREZ

THE ANGEL OF GOLIAD

TRACIE EGAN

rosen central
Primary Source™

The Rosen ~~Publishing Group, Inc.~~ New York

Published in 2004 by The Rosen Publishing Group, Inc.
29 East 21st Street, New York, NY 10010

First Edition

Library of Congress Cataloging-in-Publication Data

Egan, Tracie.
Francisca Alvarez, the Angel of Goliad / Tracie Egan.— 1st ed.
    p. cm. — (Primary sources of famous people in American history)
Includes bibliographical references (p.   ) and index.
Summary: Profiles a Mexican woman who saved more than twenty Texan rebels taken prisoner during the Texas Revolution from being shot under General Santa Anna's orders.
ISBN 0-8239-4109-4 (library binding)
ISBN 0-8239-4181-7 (pbk.)
6-pack ISBN 0-8239-4308-9
1. Alvarez, Francisca—Juvenile literature. 2. Goliad Massacre, Goliad, Tex., 1836—Juvenile literature. 3. Women heroes—Texas—Goliad—Biography—Juvenile literature. 4. Women—Mexico—Biography—Juvenile literature.
[1. Alvarez, Francisca. 2. Goliad Massacre, Goliad, Tex., 1836. 3. Women heroes. 4. Mexicans—Texas. 5. Women—Biography. 6. Texas—History—Revolution, 1835–1836.]
I. Title: Francisca Alvarez. II. Title. III. Series.
F390.A35E35 2003
976.4'03—dc21

                                                                          2002153973

Manufactured in the United States of America

Photo credits: cover, p. 5 (top) Courtesy of Mission Espiritu Santo, Goliad State Park, Texas Parks and Wildlife Department, photos by Dallas Hoppestad; p. 4 © SuperStock, Inc.; pp. 5 (bottom), 10, 27, 28 Presidio La Bahia, Goliad, Texas, photos by Dallas Hoppestad; pp. 7, 11 Library of Congress Geography and Map Division; pp. 9, 13, 18, 21, 23, 25 courtesy of Texas State Library and Archives Commission; p. 14 © The Rosen Publishing Group; p. 15 Broadsides Collection, Earl Vandale Collection, Center for American History, University of Texas at Austin; p. 16 Institute for Texan Culture at UTSA. No. 76-27; p. 17 Print Collection, Miriam and Ira D. Wallach Division of Art, Prints, and Photographs, The New York Public Library, Astor, Lenox, and Tilden Foundations; pp. 19, 29 Dallas Historical Society; p. 20 courtesy of Fannin Battle Ground SHS, Texas Parks and Wildlife Department, photo by Dallas Hoppestad; p. 22 Library of Congress Prints and Photographs Division, HABS, TEX, 88-GOLI, 4-1; p. 26 photo by Dallas Hoppestad.

Designer: Thomas Forget; Photo Researcher: Rebecca Anguin-Cohen

CONTENTS

1   WIFE OF CAPTAIN TELESFORO ALVAREZ

Francisca Alvarez was a Mexican woman who is remembered as an American hero. She saved the lives of more than 20 Texans in the Goliad Massacre. For this, she is known as the Angel of Goliad.

It is not known when or where in Mexico Francisca was born. Her family history and her childhood are also mysteries. At some point she was nicknamed Panchita.

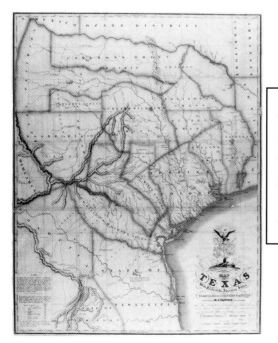

A map of Texas prepared in 1837 by Stephen Austin outlining land grants given to settlers. At this time, 14,000 families were settled there.

Above, the mural on the wall of Mission Espíritu Santo, a small church near Goliad, Texas, depicting the Goliad Massacre, among other historical scenes. Below, a painting of Mexican soldiers guarding American captives at the entrance to Presidio La Bahia.

Sometime between 1834 and 1835, when she was thought to be in her late teens or early twenties, Francisca became a close companion of Captain Telesforo Alvarez. Francisca and Alvarez lived as a married couple. Although there is no record of a legal marriage, Francisca was known as Alvarez's wife.

AN UNIDENTIFIED HEROINE

The Angel of Goliad's first name is recorded differently as Francita, Francisca, Panchita, or Pancheta, and her surname as Alavéz, Alvarez, or Alevesco. Her real surname and place of birth are not known.

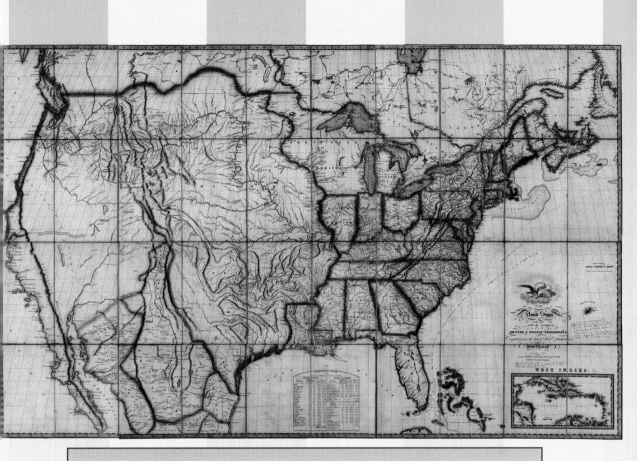

A map of the United States drawn by John Melish in 1816. As Americans moved westward, they coveted Spanish territories. Mexico established its independence from Spain in 1810.

Captain Alvarez was a commander of Mexican forces during the Texas Revolution. Captain Alvarez was born around 1803. He was from the Mexican town of Toluca. His legitimate wife was Maria Agustina de Pozo. He abandoned her in 1834, leaving her with two small children.

DID YOU KNOW?

Antonio Lopez de Santa Anna was elected president of Mexico in 1833, but soon repudiated the Mexican constitution and became a dictator. His actions pushed Americans living in Texas to fight for independence.

The flag of the independent Republic of Texas, designed in 1839. Under this flag, Texans defended the Alamo.

Francisca followed Captain Alvarez around Mexico and southern Texas while he carried out his military assignments. They traveled through Copano Bay, Goliad, Victoria, and Matamoros. She gained a reputation for aiding Texan prisoners who were captured by the Mexican army.

The courtyard of Presidio La Bahia, where Colonel Fannin's men were held before execution.

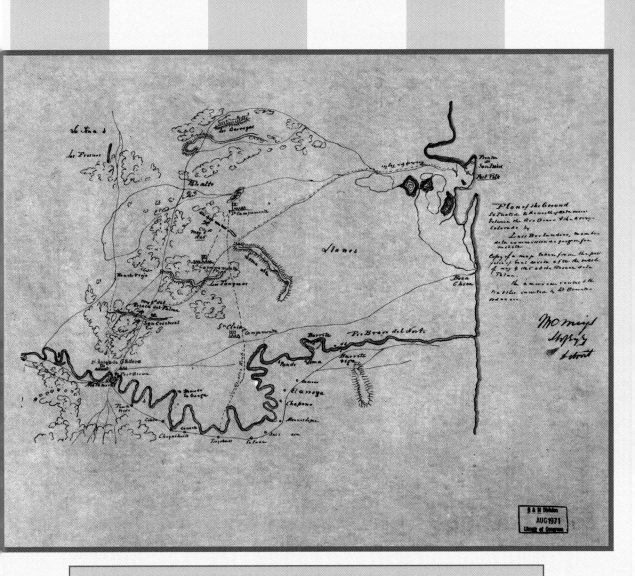

A copy of a map taken from a Mexican general showing the American routes of advance during the campaign that resulted in the capture of Colonel Fannin's troops.

2 THE TEXAS REVOLUTION

At this time in history, Texas was fighting for independence from Mexico. Texas was not yet part of the United States. The colonists of Texas wished to set up their own republic. But Mexico wanted control of Texas. It was a very bloody war, but eventually the colonists of Texas won their revolution.

DID YOU KNOW?

The Mexican American War lasted from 1846 to 1848. As a result of the American victory, California and other territories became part of the United States.

The Battle of San Jacinto, April 21, 1836. Led by Sam Houston, the Texans defeated Santa Anna's troops, and with this victory they secured their independence.

The Goliad Massacre is one of the most famous events of the Texas Revolution. General Antonio López de Santa Anna asked for and received a decree from the Mexican Congress that all foreigners bearing arms against Mexico and taken as prisoners should be shot.

Early in their struggle for independence, the Texans used this flag, daring the Mexicans to seize their lands.

UNANIMOUS

DECLARATION OF INDEPENDENCE,

BY THE

DELEGATES OF THE PEOPLE OF TEXAS,

IN GENERAL CONVENTION,

AT THE TOWN OF WASHINGTON,

ON THE SECOND DAY OF MARCH, 1836.

RICHARD ELLIS, *President.*

The Texas Declaration of Independence, adopted on March 2, 1836, declared Texas a free and independent republic.

After losing the Battle of Coleto Creek, Texas colonel James W. Fannin and his troops were out of food, water, and ammunition. They had no choice but to surrender to Mexican forces. General José de Urrea stated that Fannin and his men would be treated in a civilized manner as prisoners of war.

A portrait of Antonio López de Santa Anna, president of Mexico and commander in chief of its armed forces

PL. 6.   XIX.e siècle

COSTUMES MEXICAINS.
Dragon. Troupe de Ligne.

A Mexican dragoon, a cavalry officer. The uniforms and weapons shown here would be obsolete by the time of the Civil War.

17

Fannin and his troops, more than 300 men, gave up their weapons and surrendered. When General Santa Anna heard about the agreement between Urrea and Fannin, he ordered that Urrea follow the decree of the Mexican Congress and shoot Fannin's troops.

A list of those killed during the Goliad Massacre, prepared by Dr. Joseph H. Barnard, who was himself captured at Goliad but spared to care for the wounded

A portrait of James Walker Fannin Jr., commander of the men who were massacred at Goliad

3 THE ANGEL OF GOLIAD

When Francisca arrived at Goliad with Captain Alvarez, the Texan rebels had just been taken prisoner. The men's wrists had been tightly bound with cords. They had been forced to stand this way for hours, without water or food. Francisca's heart went out to them.

The monument that commemorates the Goliad Massacre, located in the Fannin Battle Ground State Historical Site, Texas

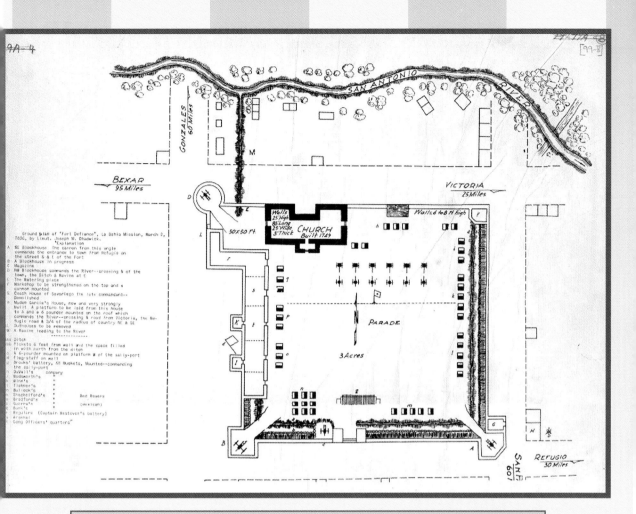

A map of Mission La Bahia, where Fannin and his men were taken after their defeat

Francisca had the cords removed from the men's wrists. She made sure that they had something to drink. She treated them with kindness when no one else would. The next morning, Francisca discovered that the men were to be killed. She pleaded with military officers until they agreed to spare the lives of twenty doctors, interpreters, nurses, and mechanics.

Mission La Bahia, where the Goliad Massacre took place. Fannin and his men were confined here for a week before being shot.

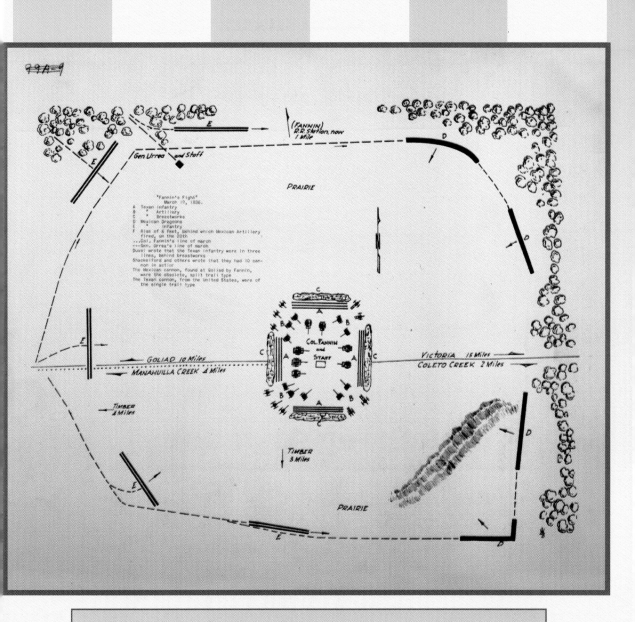

A sketch of the fortifications Colonel Fannin established at the Battle of Coleto Creek, before he ran out of ammunition and had to surrender

On the morning of March 27, 1836, the prisoners were marched out of town. At a certain spot along the way, the group was stopped. The guards fired at the prisoners at close range. Most were killed right away. Those who were not killed were pursued and slaughtered.

THE DRUMMER BOY

Benjamin F. Hughes was one of the Texans whose life was spared at the Goliad Massacre by Francisca Alvarez. He was a 15-year-old drummer boy. He lived to become a prominent citizen of Dallas.

INV 2404

Statement of I. C. Duval.

Genl Santa Anna and Genl Urrea also
I have understood, after their return to
Mexico, in order to palliate their in-
human butchery of four hundred un-
armed prisoners at Goliad, asserted
"that Col Fannin and his men had
Surrendered "unconditionally."

(TX) I will state as briefly, as possible
and to the best of my reccollection. what
occurred the morning after the battle
at the Coletto creek.

The morning after the battle of
Coletto creek, Col Fannin and his men
were Surrounded on the open prairie
by an overwhelming force of the enemy
They had formed their line of battle, and
fired several rounds of grape and can-
nister from their artillery at our en-

J-22-1

The statement prepared by John C. Duval, one of the
survivors of the massacre, describing the battle and the
events that followed

25

Francisca also concealed several more prisoners until the shooting was over. The Texans were so grateful to her that they named her the Angel of Goliad.

After the Goliad Massacre, Francisca returned to Mexico City with Captain Alvarez. He then deserted her, leaving her penniless. After Alvarez left her, Francisca was never heard of again.

This sign marks the site of the Goliad Massacre in what is now the Fannin Battle Ground State Historical Site.

A bust of Francisca Alvarez by the sculptor
Hugo Villa, located at Presidio La Bahia

27

Francisca Alvarez felt that people should not suffer or be treated unfairly, no matter what side they were on.

The men killed at Goliad have memorials in Texas dedicated to their memory. Although there isn't a memorial to Francisca, the Angel of Goliad, she will always be remembered for her kindness and courage.

A Napoleonic era cannon, a "twelve pounder," on a primitive wooden mount. These were in use until after the Civil War.

The survivors of the Goliad Massacre seated beside a flag of the Republic of Texas

TIMELINE

1834-1835—Francisca Alvarez becomes the common-law wife of Captain Telesforo Alvarez.

December 30, 1835—The Mexican Congress directs that all rebels taken in arms against the government should be shot.

March 20, 1836—Colonel James W. Fannin surrenders.

March 27, 1836—The Goliad Massacre. More than 300 Texans are shot to death by the Mexican army. More than 20 Texans are saved because of the efforts of Francisca Alvarez.

October 1835—The Texas Revolution begins at the Battle of Gonzales.

March 19, 1836—Seven Texans are killed and 60 wounded at the Battle of Coleto Creek.

March 26, 1836—Francisca Alvarez discovers the mistreatment of the prisoners of war. She has them untied and fed.

April 21, 1836—The Texas Revolution ends with the Battle of San Jacinto.

GLOSSARY

decree (dih-KREE) An official order.

interpreter (in-TER-prih-ter) Someone who translates the meanings of words from one language to another.

massacre (MAH-sih-ker) When many people are killed at one time.

memorial (meh-MOR-ee-uhl) A statute or structure established in memory of a person or group of people.

rebel (REH-bul) A person who fights against authority.

revolution (reh-vuh-LOO-shun) When people decide to overthrow a government.

WEB SITES

Due to the changing nature of Internet links, the Rosen Publishing Group, Inc., has developed an online list of Web sites related to the subject of this book. This site is updated regularly. Please use this link to access the list:

http://www.rosenlinks.com/fpah/falv

PRIMARY SOURCE IMAGE LIST

Page 4: Map of Texas prepared by Stephen Austin in 1837.
Page 5 (top): Mural at Mission Espíritu Santo, Goliad, Texas.
Page 7: Map of the United States drawn in 1816 by John Melish.
Page 9: Flag of the Republic of Texas.
Page 11: Map taken from General Arista, 1846, prepared by Luis Berlandier.
Page 16: Engraving of Santa Anna, from the *Album Mejicano*, published by C. L Prudhomme, 1843.
Page 17: Mexican dragoon, from *Costumes Civils, Militaires, et Religieux du Mexique*, Brussels, 1828, now with the New York Public Library.
Page 18: Dr. Joseph H. Barnard's list of Fannin's men.
Page 23: Sketch of Fannin's fortifications.
Page 25: Statement of John C. Duval.
Page 29: Survivors of the Goliad Massacre, from the Dallas Historical Society.

INDEX

ABOUT THE AUTHOR

Tracie Egan is a freelance writer who lives in New York City.